Texas Speak

Advanced Course

By Jennifer Briggs

Texas
Speak

[Above: Texas Speak, copyright page]

INTRODUCTION

THIS IS YOUR GRADUATE STUDY IN TEX LEX, THE LEXICON AND LORE OF THE LONE STAR STATE.

Oh, you can talk about your Southern phrases but that tourism campaign a few years ago got it down pat by calling Texas "A whole 'nother country."

This writer is a sixth generation Texan, but if you count Mamaw Kate who was said to be half American Indian, it goes back even further.

Native Texans are more Texan than, say, native Ohioans are Ohioans. And they'll let you know that the mother of their Aunt Pearl, as in this writer's Aunt Pearl, was scalped by Indians on what is now a busy boulevard of Arlington, a suburb between Fort Worth and Dallas.

Much of Texas, in spirit if not in bricks and mortar, has escaped the cultural homogenization, some call it the "McDonaldization," of the rest of the country.

Texas English has not escaped change. Fewer Texans, however, pray to the "Lard," or "warsh" their clothes, says Dr. Guy Bailey, formerly of the University of Texas at San Antonio.

According to Bailey and other scholars, however, the Lone Star twang and drawl are alive and well.

6

"It seems more and more Texans," linguist Jan Tillery told *Texas Monthly*, "are holding onto their heritage through language."

And newcomers, even recovering Yankees, who make it south of the Red River, pick up Texasisms like "fixin' to" and "y'all." Fewer pick up "might could," as in, "I might could run down to the Dairy Queen if y'all like," or "hep" for "help," "mah for "my," "awl bidness" for the "oil business."

But Texasspeak is alive an well among many of those who grew up in the state. Sometimes they'll turn it on and off, depending with whom they're visiting with on the phone. (Yes, you can visit on the phone in Texas.)

As the *Handbook of Texas* says, "Texans are, with rare exceptions, proud of their identity as Texans, a fact that is reflected in their speech." So why try to understand Texasspeak?

An anonymous writer said it best, when he put pen to paper and explained just why Texas is as much a state of mind as it is a very big landmass providing ballast for the rest of the country:

"Did you ever hear anyone go into a restaurant and say, `Wow, so you're from Oklahoma. Tell me about it'?

"Texas is the Alamo -- 183 men standing in a church facing thousands of Mexican soldiers, fighting for their freedom. We send our kids to schools named William B. Travis and Bowie, and do you know why? Because those men saw a line in the sand and they decided to be heroes ...

8

"Texas is Texas Independence day and Juneteenth... Texas is Mexican food like nowhere in the world, even Mexico.

"Texas is larger than life legends like Earl Campbell and Nolan Ryan, Denton Cooley and Michael DeBakey, Lyndon Johnson, Willie Nelson and Buddy Holly...

"Texas is huge herds of cattle and miles of crops. Texas is the best barbecue anywhere... Texas was its own country. Every time I think of all these things I tear up."

This small little book will help make comprehensible the Lone Star mindset; poet Carl Sandburg called it a "blend of valor and swagger".

It might explain why this writer automatically replied "Texas," whenever asked country of origin by a U.S. Customs lady after a flight from Canada.

And, in a more practical way, *Texas Speak Advance Course* will keep you from fitting a boot in your mouth, and without stepping in a pile of something fresh first.

CHAPTER I

QUICK REVIEW

Before proceeding to new territory,

here's a catch-up on basic Texan.

One thing visitors and newcomers

invariably get wrong is "y'all,"

which is mostly used as a *plural*,

referring to a group of folks.

That is, *except in the expression*,

"Y'allcomeback, heah?"

And that can be addressed

to a solitary individual.

Texas is so
BIG,
it's got two dialects:

The
EAST TEXAS DRAWL
and the
WEST TEXAS TWANG.

Usually, but not always,

a line dividing the state in two,

otherwise known as Interstate 35,

is a rough boundary.

But you'll find diversity of

pronunciation among natives

of the same Texas town.

Recalling the making of the hit TV series, Dallas, actor Steve Kanaly said:

"You have **eight** core actors

trying to come up with their version of a

Dallas accent,

and Texas has a huge range of accents.

In **Southwest Texas** I know

many oilmen who sound like they have a

bunch of hushpuppies in their mouth.

In **East Texas** they talk kinda fast,

kinda excited, kinda like JR."

Another Texas
expression commonly
heard reflects the
importance of making
one's acquaintance
proper like.

"We've howdied
    but we haven't shook."

When a Texan tells you,

"This ain't my first rodeo,"

he's telling you he really knows what's up.

When there's a possibility a
Texan *can* or *will do something*,
he or she will,

"I might could..."
And when it's about to happen
(maybe), the Texan says,

"I'm fixin' to..."
["I'm" is pronounced ahm.]

Fixin' means you are about to do something, could be a matter of years, as in, *"I'm fixin' to buy some property out at Lake Whitney,"* or minutes, as in, *"I'm fixin' to brush my teeth and turn on Jay Leno."*

It is also a widely used procrastination device such as in telling the household you are *"fixin' to fix supper,"* when you really are just dragging your feet, but by mentioning it out loud, you have at least signaled intent.

CHAPTER II

CARDS, GODS AND DOMINOES

In some corners of Texas,

do not bring up cards

~ the playing kind ~

unless you want your

eternal salvation questioned.

Some Texans don't even keep
a deck in the house.

Parts of Texas are the silver

buckle of the **Bible Belt**,

where cards are sinful,

"cause they lead to gambling,"

which many Texans know,

leads to dancing,

which leads to well,

you know.

But chances are there's a set or two of dominos.

Charles "Good Time Charlie" Wilson knew that.

For years an unabashedly skirt-chasing,

hard-drinking congressman, Wilson handed out boxes

of Texas-made dominos to loyal voters in his

God-fearing East Texas district.

If you bring up cards,

they better be from Hallmark,

telling you how sorry

they are your

meemaw was called

to the hereafter.

*Which brings up
the matter of death.
It just isn't done
among
God-fearing folk.*

If you live in
Texas, you better
not die.

You'd best *"pass away"*

or **even better,**

"passed into the arms of her

loving maker,"

"passed into eternal rest in the

arms of the Lord,"

or even, and

this actually

appeared in a Texas newspaper,

"gone fishing with Jesus."

If you are Jewish, just lie.

The Lord'll know the difference by the hairstyle.

If they had to squish it to get it in the
casket with a hay baler, then he'll know to stick
you in that great Baptist pneumatic tube.

*Speaking of religion, one hot Texas summer
prompted an ecumenical wag to say:*

"It's so dry the Baptists are sprinkling,
the Methodists are spitting, and the Catholics
are giving rain checks."

Songwriter Butch Hancock said
of growing up in the Lone Star Bible Belt:

"Life in Lubbock,

Texas,

taught me two things:

One is that God loves you

and you're going to burn

in hell. The other is that

sex is the most awful,

filthy thing on earth

and you should **save** it for

someone you love."

CHAPTER III

YOU KNOW YOU'RE IN TEXAS WHEN...

The date is told,

"You sure clean up good."

And she's flattered!

The judge wears judicial robes

and snakeskin boots.

Summer is followed by more summer,

still summer, and Christmas.

The thermostat
is switched
from
A/C to *heat*
and back
on the
same day.

Stores don't have **bags**;
they have **sacks**.

*Mourners wear bib
overalls at funerals.*

Kids find themselves
trick-or-treating in
90-degree heat.

People argue over whose
mother made
the best breakfast
consisting of a hunk
of bread with
flavored flour water,
a **delicacy** otherwise
known as
"biscuits 'n gravy".

Bridges, or rivers, are not
necessarily associated with water.

A customized pickup

prompts more

jealous murmurs than

a Mercedes, and is

just as welcome at

fancy French restaurants

and posh country clubs.

Hot water comes out
of both taps in August.

The café utilizes five spices:
**salt, pepper, Ranch dressing,
BBQ sauce** and **ketchup.**

The preacher says,
*"I'd like to ask Bubba to help
take up the offering."*
And five men stand up.

CHAPTER VI

TEXAS BRAGGADOCIO, TEXAS STUPID

Lone Star
state residents have
a reputation for
bragging on themselves,
but it can cut
both ways.

*Some will try to
outdo others with the
alleged humbleness of
their beginnings, by saying:*

~ ~ ~ ~ ~ ~ ~ ~ ~ ~ ~ ~ ~ ~ ~ ~

"I ate so many armadillos

when I was young I still

roll up into a ball when

I hear a dog bark."

"We were so
poor my brother
and me had to
ride double on
our stick horse."

"If a trip
around the world
cost a dollar,
I couldn't get to
the Oklahoma line."

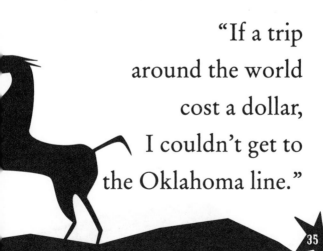

"I was so poor

I had a tumbleweed

as a pet."

We're not claiming that every Texan is the sharpest knife in the drawer.

Actress Janine Turner,
who grew up around Arlington,
once said:

"You can take the girl out of Texas but not the Texas out of the girl and ultimately not the girl out of Texas." Well, OK.

*An all-purpose
Texas description
of an idiot:*
"That boy's so
dumb he couldn't
pour piss out of
a boot unless the
instructions were
printed on
the bottom."

*And that governor-turned-
president, George W. Bush, once
explained to the uninitiated:*
"Some folks look at me and see a
certain swagger, which in Texas
is called 'walking.'"

*Ma Ferguson, who succeeded
Pa Ferguson as governor in the
1920s, once said with complete
confidence in her facts:*
"If the King's English was good
enough for Jesus, it's good
enough for me."

CHAPTER V

DEFINITION BREAK

- **Wore out or wear out.**

  This is something that can happen to jeans, or a person after a long workday. But generally in Texas, if you hear a mother hollering, *"I am gonna wear you out,"* chasing behind a screeching, guilty-looking child, it means a big spanking is about to happen.

- **Hind legs of destruction.**

  A personal favorite, this can mean a person or a place is in a state of shambles. Mother would walk in, see a house strewn with toys and school books and bowls that had to be returned after the First Baptist potluck, and pronounce, *"This house looks like the hind legs of destruction."* Or, she would look herself in the mirror when her bouffant boost was still two days away, and, hair pick in hand, declare, *"My hair looks like the hind legs of destruction."*

- **The house was seven ways for Sunday, or the house was every way for Christmas.**

  A holy mess.

• Aint

Yes, we all know Texans and other Southerners say *"ain't,"* as a substitute for *"not."* But in Texas, we have a different kind of aint. No apostrophe necessary. Your aint makes you chocolate meringue pies and is married to your uncle. Your aint is your mamma's sister or you daddy's sister, or sometimes just a cousin your mamma's age to where it feels funny not to address her as *"aint."*

• Went to hunt the...

This old timey expression is still used today. Let's say, for instance, I give my father a real nice beach umbrella for Christmas to stick in his outdoor furniture. The first warm days of spring pop up, and where in the heck did daddy put that umbrella? Had he put it at the curb with the Christmas tree? Then, a few weeks later, mother's car keys are nowhere to be found. Finally, in sheer exhaustion, she plops on the couch and says, "Well, I guess they went to hunt the umbrella."

• Walk off.

This expression is generally saved for the couch or dining room table that has accumulated too much stuff. A mother walks in one afternoon and sees puzzles and pots and pans and three days worth of mail and a large box of dog treats and declares, *"This table looks like it's gonna walk off."*

• A hit dog'll yelp.

Every so often, a reporter with national newspaper writing about a politician in the middle of a mud-slinging match would ask rhetorically, *"What is it they say in Texas? A hit dog'll yelp?"* Yes, that's what they say. And it's not restricted to politicos. A kid gets caught in school doing something bad and immediately begins yelping how he didn't do anything. Criminals on the TV reality show COPS gets caught with drugs on their person and start squealing like stuck pigs on account of they're guilty. Yep, a hit dog'll yelp. You mark my words.

• Steak so good you'll slap your grandmother.

A particularly succulent beefsteak, can be applied to any food with the possible exception of herring or other patently Yankee vittles, which is what Texans call victuals.

- ## Didn't go to.

  This is a real simple apologetic expression that says, *"I didn't mean to."* Some people even say it to their dogs when they step on their tail. *"Oh, baby, I didn't go to."* In other words, *"I didn't set out to do it."* Can only be used in more minor situations, when you've messed up your kid's t-shirt in the wash, or maybe thrown away the TIME magazine before your spouse has gotten to read it.

- ## Dadgum.

  There are several substitutes for mild swear words, but this seems to be most popular as far as the, *"damn,"* family of epithets goes.

- ## Cuter than a speckled pup.

  This, ladies, is really a compliment, often heard late in the bars of west Texas before the lights go up.

- ## Ear screws.

  Sounds like a horrendous form of primitive torture, but to Texans they are just earrings.

ON THE RANCH:

Cow: a female bovine

Heifer: pronounced, heff-ur, a female bovine that hasn't given birth, or calved.

Calf: a young bovine of either gender

Bull: adult male bovine

Steer: an emasculated bovine, whose missing appendage, if rolled in corn meal and chicken-fried, becomes a delicacy called calf fries.

Cattle: plural for any of the above

Herd: a mess of cattle

Ranchette: any piece of Texas land with four-legged critters and less than 1,000 acres.

AND REMEMBER:

Don't kick a cow chip on a hot day.

Don't drink downstream from the herd.

Don't squat with your spurs on.

WEATHER DESCRIPTIONS:

Colder than a mother-in-law's kiss: cold

Blue Norther: very cold

Gully washer: heavy downpour

Terd floater: heavier downpour

So dry the birds
are building their nests
out of barbed wire.

So dry the catfish

are carrying canteens.

So dry the trees
are bribing the dogs

It's been dry so long
we only got a quarter inch of rain
during Noah's flood.

So dry I'm spitting cotton.

So hot the hens are laying
hard-boiled eggs.

Hot as a summer revival.

"We don't have a climate

in Texas,

but we've got plenty

of weather

to make up for it."

CHAPTER VI

POLITICS
AND
SCHOOL TIES

In Texas, there are dominoes,
Friday night football and politics.

As columnist Molly Ivins says,

"Good thing we've still

got politics in Texas -

finest form of

free entertainment

ever invented."

With politicians like LBJ, Ann Richards, Jim Hightower and George W. "Shrub" Bush, you know politics Texas-style is going to be different.

*Former Gov. Richards'
punditry includes:*

"I've always said that in politics,
your enemies can't hurt you,
but your friends will kill you."

And there's sage political advice from Texas,

applicable in any state:

"Never wrestle with a pig, you both get muddy and the pig just likes it."

You may not always agree with Hightower,

Texas' outspokenly liberal former

agriculture commissioner. But it's hard to

find a better-aimed quotesmith.

"When I entered politics," he has said,
"I took the only downward turn you could take from journalism."

"Politics isn't about left versus right; it's about top versus bottom." One thing for sure, Hightower has never been accused of being non-partisan.

"The middle of the road is for yellow lines and dead armadillos," Hightower has said on more than one occasion, as he has:

"Republicans are so empty-headed, they wouldn't make a good landfill."

Also pure-de Hightower: "Even a little dog can piss on a big building. Or: "A little ol' boy in the Panhandle told me the other day you can still make a small fortune in agriculture. Problem is, you got to start with a large one."

Speaking of agriculture, Jim has said: "The only difference between a pigeon and the American farmer today is that a pigeon can still make a deposit on a John Deere."

And: "The Bible declares that on the sixth day God created man. Right then and there, God should have demanded a damage deposit."

Some complain Texans
don't always get their priorities right.

Former Gov. Mark White once famously griped:

"The rest of the world is sweeping past us. The oil and gas of the Texas future is the well-educated mind. But we are still wor-ried about whether Midland can beat Odessa at football. "

As for politicians, Molly Ivins believes they have their own special perspective:

"As they say around the Texas Legislature, 'if you can't drink their whiskey, screw their women, take their money, and vote against 'em anyway, you don't belong in office.' "

LBJ had a low opinion of some fellow politicians, famously saying of one:

"He's so dumb, he doesn't know whether it's raining or someone's pissing on his boots."

He obviously didn't know the old Texas saying, "One who slings dirt, loses ground."

Another saying of Texas political wisdom goes:

"Don't publicly ally yourself with the guys who are being burned in effigy by the local mob."

School Lore

There are several fine schools in Texas, but probably none more storied than **Texas A&M University in College Station. They are Aggies.**

You must know that their big rivals are the **Texas Longhorns of the University of Texas in Austin.** For over 100 years they have been playing sports and painting or stealing each other's mascots.

Bevo is the steer from UT. He's harder to make off with.

Reveille is a little dog at A&M who is never to be away from her handler, and supposedly is permitted entry wherever her cadet goes in College Station.

There are Aggie jokes (UT jokes have never caught on for some reason), and most people explain it by saying they are akin to Polish jokes.

For example:

Know how to tell the Aggie on an offshore oil rig?

"He's the one throwin' bread at the helicopters."

Aggies deny doing goofy things, then turn around and start cloning pet cats, or welcome the George Bush Presidential Library to their campus.

And they have their own Aggie joke:

What do you call an Aggie 10 years after graduating?

"Boss."

And when Lyle Lovett, the singer and an Aggie, was asked his favorite Aggie joke, replied:

"Sorry, I don't understand the question."

Texas lawyers can be something else too.

When Dick DeGuerin, a liberal Democrat lawyer and friend of Nicaragua Sandinista leader Daniel Ortega, isn't busy defending serial killers, David Koresh or conservative Republicans like Tom DeLay for the professional challenge, he lectures at the University of Texas at Austin Law School, his alma mater.

DeGuerin recites in class that old Texas saying to explain why some **certain hombres have a date with the noose:**

"No horse ever needed stealing --
but there are people who need killing."

CHAPTER VII

More Definition and Usage

• Wrench

Not something you fix your car with. A wrench is something you put on your hair to hide whatever color the Lord gave you that you dislike.

• Fixins

This is stuff that goes with food. Not just pickles and deviled eggs, but everything but the entrée.

• Go to the house

It can be said at the end of a workday, or the end of a bar night. "I'm goin' to the house," is applicable in any case where you have decided -- or are allowed to -- exit.

• Law law

This is to keep from saying, "Lord," or "Lordy, Lordy," or, 'Oh good gawd," any of which could be considered on the level of card playin', or cheatin' at the dominoes game, 42. Texans do not take the Lord's name in vain, unless stopped for drunk driving.

- ## I'll Swan

  This is another one that keeps you from cussing. It means, "I'll swear," like one might say if seeing a parakeet riding a capuchin monkey down your driveway in the low light of the neighbor's stadium-style security system.

- ## Supper

  Usually the evening meal, but could be noon, could be 3 p.m. We have supper when we want it. Usually any main meal after breakfast.

EVERYDAY TEXAS EXPRESSIONS

Happy as a gopher in soft dirt.

Well, why wouldn't he be?

Are you goin' to the ballgame?

You just assume this is something that happens Friday, about 7 p.m. And no liquor is allowed -- unless, of course, it's poured in McDonald's cups.

She's got tongue enough for 10 rows of teeth

The woman is not close-mouthed.

Ridin' the gravy train with biscuit wheels.

Can apply anyone who wins the lottery, or moves up the corporate ladder for reasons no one can explain -- except at the bar later.

They ate supper before saying grace.

Refers to enjoying honeymoon pleasures before securing a wedding license or ceremony.

He's got a big hole in his screen door.

He's stupid, as in:
The porch light's on but no one is home.

Time to paint your butt white and run with the antelope.

An admonition to stop prevaricating and join up.

Rollin' ball o' butcher knives

A favorite phrase of a former Dallas Cowboys football coach, as in, "That boy is a rollin' ball of butcher knives," meaning the person is a mess – in a good or interesting way.

I wonder what poor people eat.

Popularized during the Depression, used to praise a big spread on the dinner table.

She wouldn't give you snow water if it was snowin'.

To describe a tightwad.

When a Texan's business is good, he or she is:

Busy as a hound in flea season.
Panting like a lizard on a hot rock.
Busy as a funeral home fan in July.

CHAPTER VIII

TEXAS INSULTS, TEXAS WISDOM

"He's so country he thinks a seven course meal is a possum and a six pack."

"There are a lot of nooses in his family tree."

"He looks like 10 miles of bad road."

"He'd argue with a wooden Indian."

"She's two sandwiches short of a picnic."

"Tighter than a power line after a blue norther."

"Faster than a duck on a June bug."

"He's a bubble off plumb."

"He was born tired and
since suffered a relapse."

"He's crooked as the Brazos."

**"He's so ugly his mama used to have to
tie a pork chop around his neck to get
the dogs to play with him."**

"She's thin as a bar of soap after a hard day's washin."

"I can explain it to you but
I can't understand it for you."

"Crazy as an acre of snakes."

"He's as confused as a cow on astroturf."

Texas Wisdom

"Never slap a man who's
chewin' tobacco."

"Good judgment comes from experi-
ence, and a lot of that comes
from bad judgment."

"If you get to thinkin' you're a person
of some influence, try orderin'
somebody else's dog around."

"If you find yourself in a hole, the first thing to do is stop diggin'."

"A worm is the only animal that can't fall down."

"You can't get lard unless you boil the hog."

"Don't hang your wash on someone else's line."

73

"Never miss a good chance to shut up."

74

"You dance with them
that brung ya."

"It ain't bragging
if you can do it."

"The guilty dog barks
first and loudest."

"You can't win a puking
contest with a buzzard."

"If you can't improve on a story, there's no sense in retelling it."

"You can put your boots in the oven but that don't make 'em biscuits." This expression sometimes substitutes "butt" for "boots," depending on present company.

"If you give a lesson in meanness to a critter [or a person], don't be surprised if they learn that lesson."

Tired of the expression,
"Don't cry over spilled milk"?

Try the Texas version:
"It doesn't matter how much milk you spill as long as you don't lose your cow."

"When you get to the end of your rope, tie a knot in it and hang on."

"Don't let the screen door hit ya' where the good Lord split ya'!"

"You don't bring a knife to a gun fight."

"If all you ever **do**
is all you've ever **done,**
then all you'll **get**
is all you've ever **got.**"

*"Even the sun shines
on a dog's ass sometimes."*

"Only fools argue with
skunks, mules, or cooks."

" If **one** person tells you,

you are a **horse's rear**, *forget it.*

If **two** people tell you that you are

a **horse's rear,** *look in the mirror.*

But if **three** people tell you

that you are a **horse's rear,**

buy a saddle. "

JENNIFER BRIGGS

is a freelance writer and author in Fort Worth. Her ancestors helped establish Texas, as well as threw dead cats in passing vehicles on Halloween. Jennifer began working at the *Fort Worth Star-Telegram* at 18, fresh off a stint as the very first Texas Rangers ball girl. For seven years, she assumed the persona of pro-wrestling columnist Betty Ann Stout. She later covered the Philadelphia Phillies and Green Bay Packers for other newspapers. She also has worked in radio.

Her books include, *Quotable Billy Graham, The Book of Landry, Strive to Excel: The will and wisdom of Vince Lombardi, A Very Brady Guide to Life, Nolan Ryan: The Authorized Pictorial History.* Her stories have twice been included in the anthology, *Best American Sportwriting.* She and husband Mike live in Texas with three large dogs who eat windows.